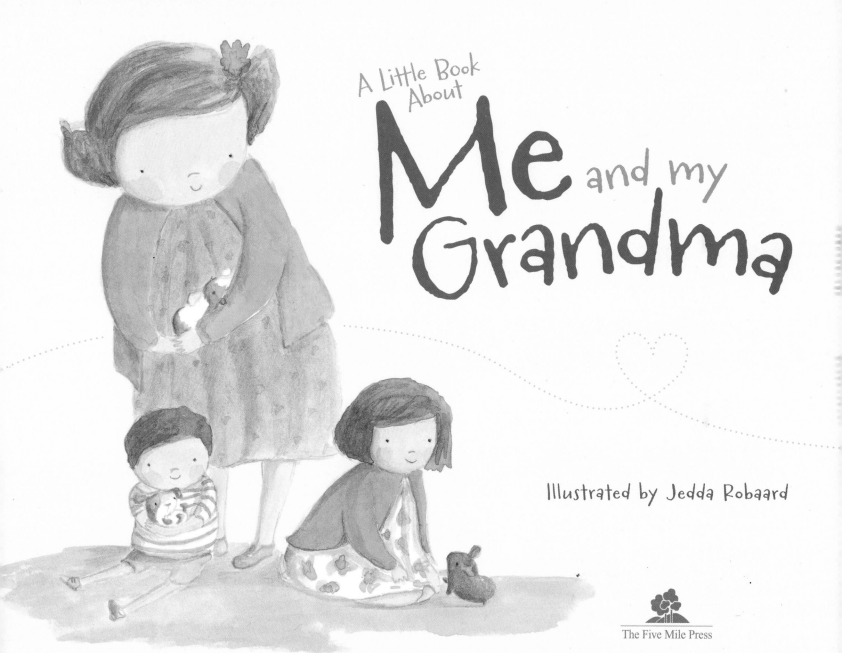

A Little Book
About

Me and my
Grandma

Illustrated by Jedda Robaard

The Five Mile Press

This is a book to fill in and share with your grandma.
You may need some help to complete it – that's what grandmas are for!
You can use the pouch in the back of the book to store photographs,
postcards, birthday cards, and anything else that is special to you and your grandma.
Write a special message for your grandma in the gift card provided.

The Five Mile Press Pty Ltd
1 Centre Road, Scoresby
Victoria 3179 Australia
www.fivemile.com.au

CIP data is available from the
National Library of Australia

First published 2012

Printed in China 5 4 3 2 1

This is my grandma and me.

Draw or attach a photo of you and your grandma here.

Grandma was born in a place called
....

Now she lives in a place called
....

I live in a place called
....

Mark these places on the map.

My grandma's mum

is called

....

She is my great-grandma!

Me

Mum

Siblings

Dad

Grandparents

Grandparents

Great-grandparents

Great-grandparents

My Family

Fill in your
family tree.

When grandma was little,

her favourite games were

Grandma and I love playing games.
Our best game is

....

....

....

....

When grandma was young,

she had a pet ....

called ....

I have a pet ....

called ....

Our pets never met – but here is a picture of both of them!

Draw a picture ↑
of your pets here.

When grandma was little,

she wanted to be a ....

When I grow up, I want to be a ....

Here is a picture of my grandma dressed as a ....

She looks beautiful / scary / happy / fierce!

Draw a costume on grandma.

Grandma's
favourite
colour is

....

My favourite colour is

....

Here are some flowers in our favourite colours

Draw
and colour
in the
flowers.

When we are together,
grandma
and I love to eat.

Our favourite foods

Make a list or draw your favourite foods here.

For my birthday,
grandma
likes to make

....

My favourite birthday present from grandma was ....

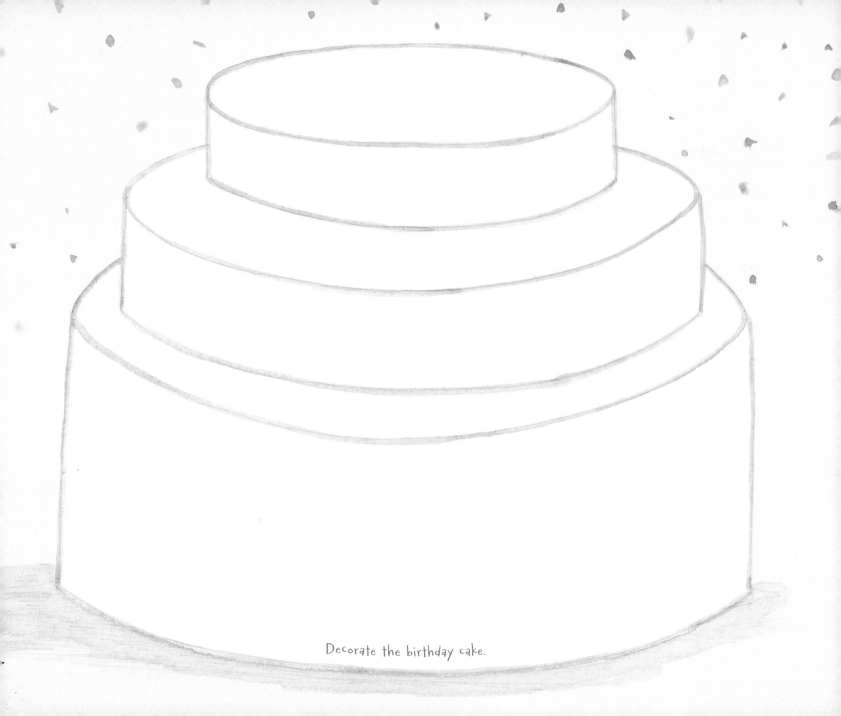

Decorate the birthday cake.

Grandma loves going on holidays.

Her favourite holiday was

....

The best place grandma and I have been together is

....

Draw or attach a photo of you
and your grandma on holidays. ↗

Grandma's favourite book is

My favourite book is

Grandma's favourite story to read to me is

I love my grandma.

That's why I've made this special book and card just for her!